See It Grow!

by Lili Henderson

See the pot.
The pot is big.

Feel the soil.
The soil is damp.

See the seeds.
The seeds are small.

Feel the water.
The water is wet.

Feel the sun.
The sun is hot.

See the leaves.
The leaves are green.

See the tomatoes.
The tomatoes are sweet.